W9-AWO-812

U.S. PRESIDENTIAL ELECTIONS: HOW THEY WORK

PRESIDENTIAL CAMPAIGNS

LISA A. MCPARTLAND

PowerKiDS
press.

New York

Published in 2020 by The Rosen Publishing Group, Inc.
29 East 21st Street, New York, NY 10010

Copyright © 2020 by The Rosen Publishing Group, Inc.

All rights reserved. No part of this book may be reproduced in any form without permission in writing from the publisher, except by a reviewer.

First Edition

Editor: Rachel Gintner
Book Design: Tanya Dellaccio

Photo Credits: Cover Alex Wong/Getty Images News/Getty Images; p. 5 Everett Historical/Shutterstock.com; p. 7 (top) Photo 12/Universal Images Group/Getty Images; p. 7 (bottom) https://upload.wikimedia.org/wikipedia/commons/b/b6/Gilbert_Stuart_Williamstown_Portrait_of_George_Washington.jpg; p. 9 (top) Nerthuz/Shutterstock.com; p. 9 (bottom) https://upload.wikimedia.org/wikipedia/commons/3/38/Thomas_H_Nast.jpg; pp. 10, 11 JEFF KOWALSKY/AFP/Getty Images; p. 13 (top) Chip Somodevilla/Getty Images News/Getty Images; p. 13 (bottom) David Hume Kennerly/Archive Photos/Getty Images; p. 15 (top) https://upload.wikimedia.org/wikipedia/commons/c/c4/Bass_Otis_%28American%2C_1784-1861%29_-_Portrait_of_William_Henry_Harrison.jpg; p. 15 (bottom) Universal History Archive/Universal Images Group/Getty Images; p. 17 (top) DNetromphotos/Shutterstock.com; pp. 17 (bottom), 28 ROBYN BECK/AFP/Getty Images; p. 19 NurPhoto/Getty Images; p. 20 https://upload.wikimedia.org/wikipedia/commons/1/12/George_Edwin_Taylor.jpg; p. 21 https://upload.wikimedia.org/wikipedia/commons/7/71/Victoria_Woodhull_by_Mathew_Brady_c1870.png; p. 22 AFP/Getty Images; p. 23 Rick Friedman/Corbis Historical/Getty Images; p. 25 Brooks Kraft/Corbis Historical/Getty Images; p. 27 Bettmann/Getty Images; p. 29 Irfan Khan/Los Angeles Times/Getty Images.

Cataloging-in-Publication Data

Names: McPartland, Lisa A.
Title: Presidential campaigns / Lisa A. McPartland.
Description: New York : PowerKids Press, 2020. | Series: U.S. presidential elections: how they work | Includes glossary and index.
Identifiers: ISBN 9781725310865 (pbk.) | ISBN 9781725310889 (library bound) | ISBN 9781725310872 (6 pack)
Subjects: LCSH: Presidents–United States–Election–History–Juvenile literature. | Presidential candidates–United States–History–Juvenile literature. | Political campaigns–United States–History–Juvenile literature. | United States–Politics and government–Juvenile literature.
Classification: LCC E176.1 M4257 2020 | DDC 324.973–dc23

Manufactured in the United States of America

CPSIA Compliance Information: Batch # CWPK20. For Further Information contact Rosen Publishing, New York, New York at 1-800-237-9932.

CONTENTS

WHAT IS A PRESIDENTIAL CAMPAIGN?

If a candidate decides that he or she wants to be elected president of the United States, the candidate has to tell people why he or she would make a good president. But how does a candidate do this? A candidate must form a presidential campaign. A presidential campaign is started in an effort to convince voters to support one candidate over another. In this type of campaign, a candidate must tell voters what makes him or her the best person to lead the country.

A presidential campaign involves many steps, including raising and spending money, traveling around the country, and debating political opponents. Campaigns also include advertising on television, in newspapers, and through social media. This book will explore how presidential campaigns work.

Presidential campaigns are necessary to educate the public on why candidates want to be president. This poster illustrates that candidate Grover Cleveland and running mate Allen Thurman wanted lower taxes and tariffs.

UNDERSTANDING "CAMPAIGN"

Before we discuss presidential campaigns, we must understand the word "campaign." This word can be a verb or a noun. As a verb, campaign means to engage in a **crusade** for a certain cause or person. So, if a person wants to become president, he or she must be a strong **advocate** for himself or herself.

As a noun, campaign means a series of actions or events that are meant to achieve a result. So, that means a person seeking the office of President of the United States runs a presidential campaign. While we will discuss the act of campaigning, we mainly will focus on the noun form of the word. This will help us to understand what a full presidential campaign includes.

Our nation's first president, George Washington, served two terms as president, but he didn't have to campaign. He was unopposed in 1789 and 1792. The first opposed presidential race was in 1796. ▶

The first step a person must consider is whether or not he or she can legally become president. A presidential candidate must be a United States citizen. That means he or she has to have been born here. The candidate also must be 35 years old or older. Also, the candidate has to have been a United States resident for 14 years.

A person cannot be elected as president more than twice. This is called a term limit. The U.S. Constitution sets these rules. If a candidate meets these rules, then he or she can declare that they are running for president under a certain party. This is known as declaring his or her candidacy. The candidate then must create a campaign committee to build a **platform** and to raise and spend money.

PATH TO THE PRESIDENCY
A PERSON RUNNING FOR FEDERAL OFFICE MUST REGISTER AND FILE FINANCIAL REPORTS WITH THE FEDERAL ELECTION COMMISSION IF THE PERSON RAISES OR SPENDS MORE THAN $5,000.

Presidential campaigns in current times feature two main parties, Democrats and Republicans. The donkey first represented Democrats during the 1828 presidential campaign of Andrew Jackson. During his race, Jackson's opponents likened him to a donkey, so he used the symbol on his campaign posters. The elephant first was used to represent Republicans in 1874, when Thomas Nast used it in his political cartoons.

THOMAS NAST

WHY CAMPAIGNS ARE IMPORTANT

Why do politicians have to create campaigns? In **democracies**, campaigns ensure that candidates are able to fairly and equally share their platforms with potential voters. Presidential campaigns educate voters about each candidate's position on issues that are important to the entire country. Some of those issues include health care costs, the economy, foreign policy, **immigration**, and the environment. Campaigns are important because they

PATH TO THE PRESIDENCY

MANY AMERICANS THINK PEOPLE WHO GIVE LARGE AMOUNTS OF MONEY TO CANDIDATES HAVE TOO MUCH INFLUENCE OVER ELECTIONS AND POLICIES. THIS IS WHY MANY AMERICANS WANT TO LIMIT CAMPAIGN DONATIONS.

STRONGER TOGETHER
hillaryclinton.com

Campaign rallies are an important part of the presidential campaign process. A rally is a gathering where potential voters listen as candidates share their messages. Rallies also help candidates raise more money and attract more votes.

help candidates raise the money needed to run for office. Presidential elections cost billions of dollars, so each candidate spends several million dollars. When Hillary Clinton campaigned in 2016, her campaign spent $768 million. Campaigns are expensive because the candidate's message must be shared with people across the country if he or she hopes to win both the primary election and the general election.

PRIMARY AND GENERAL ELECTIONS

A primary election is a **preliminary** election in which voters of each party nominate candidates for office. Primaries were introduced in the early 1900s. Previously, candidates were all chosen by caucuses. A caucus is different than a primary. In a primary, voters directly pick the candidate they favor. In a caucus, voters choose delegates to represent the state's interests.

In presidential races, each state has its own primary race or caucus. Some states use a combination of primaries and caucuses. The primary elections are used to pick delegates for the presidential nominating conventions of the two major parties, Democrats and Republicans. Primaries serve as a measure of public opinion. This means that primaries reflect who the voters want to see run in the general election.

Party conventions are large gatherings of delegates who choose a candidate to run in the general presidential election.

For the most part, delegates to conventions are chosen proportionally to how votes were cast. So, if 50 percent of the voters favored one candidate, then 50 percent of the delegates chosen would favor that candidate. However, primary and caucus votes are not necessarily binding. This means that delegates could choose another candidate, even if most of the voters did not choose that candidate. Once each party chooses its candidate for president, those candidates campaign in the general election.

Presidential general elections occur every four years on the first Tuesday after the first Monday in November. The person who wins the most Electoral College votes wins the presidential election. The president is **inaugurated** on January 20 (or January 21 if January 20 falls on a Sunday) of the following year.

PATH TO THE PRESIDENCY

THERE ARE TWO MAIN TYPES OF PRIMARY ELECTIONS. IN CLOSED PRIMARIES, ONLY VOTERS REGISTERED TO THE PARTY CAN VOTE FOR THAT PARTY'S CANDIDATE. IN OPEN PRIMARIES, VOTERS CAN CHOOSE ANY PARTY'S CANDIDATE.

WILLIAM HENRY HARRISON

When a presidential candidate wins the general election, the winner begins his or her presidency on Inauguration Day. The nation's first president, George Washington, delivered the shortest inauguration speech at 135 words. William Henry Harrison's 1841 inauguration speech, which lasted nearly two hours, was the longest at 8,455 words.

THE ELECTORAL COLLEGE

We just learned that the person who wins the most Electoral College votes wins the presidential election. But what is the Electoral College? The Electoral College is a group chosen to cast votes for the president and vice president. Voters do not directly elect the president. Votes in a presidential election count toward a group of electors who pledge to vote for a specific candidate in the Electoral College.

Each state has a certain number of Electoral College votes. The number is based on the state's population. The presidential candidate who wins the most votes in each state wins that state's Electoral College votes. A candidate must win 270 or more Electoral College votes out of 538 to become president.

Each state has different numbers of Electoral College votes. A candidate must win 270 or more Electoral College votes to win the election. In the 2016 election, Donald Trump won 306 Electoral College votes, and Hillary Rodham Clinton won 232 votes. However, Trump did not win the popular vote. This means he did not have more overall votes than Clinton. A total of 62,984,825 people voted for Trump, but 65,853,516 people voted for Clinton.

ELECTORAL COLLEGE MAP 2016

Map labels:
12 WA | 3 MT | 3 ND | 10 MN | 10 WI | 16 MI | 3 1 ME | 4 NH | 11 MA
7 OR | 4 ID | 3 WY | 5 NE | 6 IA | 11 IN | 18 OH | 29 NY | 3 VT | 4 RI
6 NV | 3 SD | 9 CO | 6 KS | 20 IL | 5 WV | 13 VA | 20 PA | 7 CT
55 CA | 6 UT | 5 NM | 10 MO | 8 KY | 15 NC | 14 NJ
11 AR | 7 OK | 6 AR | 11 TN | 9 SC | 3 DE
38 TX | 8 LA | 6 MS | 9 AL | 16 GA | 10 MD | 3 DC
3 AK | 4 HI | 29 FL

RED = STATE'S ELECTORAL COLLEGE VOTES WENT TO TRUMP

BLUE = STATE'S ELECTORAL COLLEGE VOTES WENT TO CLINTON

ELECTORAL COLLEGE WINNERS

IT'S POSSIBLE FOR A PRESIDENTIAL CANDIDATE TO WIN THE POPULAR VOTE, MEANING THE MOST VOTES IN THE COUNTRY, BUT STILL NOT BECOME PRESIDENT. THIS IS BECAUSE THE PERSON WHO WINS THE MOST VOTES STILL MIGHT NOT WIN THE MOST ELECTORAL COLLEGE VOTES. FIVE PRESIDENTS WON THEIR ELECTIONS WITHOUT WINNING THE POPULAR VOTE: JOHN QUINCY ADAMS (1824), RUTHERFORD B. HAYES (1876), BENJAMIN HARRISON (1888), GEORGE W. BUSH (2000), AND DONALD TRUMP (2016).

WHY ELECTIONS ARE IMPORTANT

We've discussed why presidential campaigns are important, but why are elections important? Elections are important to democratic **governance** because they allow the people to vote for their leaders. The people hold elected leaders **accountable** for how they perform when they are in office. If a leader does not perform well, then voters can choose not to reelect the leader. Also, elections help to educate citizens. They allow people to have their say on issues that are important to them.

Elections also ensure that the will of the people, or what the majority of voters want, is followed. If a candidate is elected but then does something that the people do not want, the people can vote against that candidate during the next election.

Elections are important to keep democracy alive. In a democracy, voters elect candidates to serve the "will of the people," or what the voters want. Representatives include a president, a vice president, 100 senators, and 435 representatives in the House of Representatives.

THE CAMPAIGN CYCLE

PRESIDENTIAL CAMPAIGNS OFTEN BEGIN IN THE SPRING OF THE YEAR BEFORE THE ELECTION. PRIMARIES AND CAUCUSES TAKE PLACE BETWEEN THE SUMMER OF THE YEAR BEFORE THE ELECTION AND THE SPRING OF THE ELECTION YEAR. FROM JULY TO SEPTEMBER OF THE ELECTION YEAR, PARTIES CHOOSE THEIR CANDIDATES FOR THE GENERAL ELECTION. DURING SEPTEMBER AND OCTOBER OF ELECTION YEAR, THE FINAL CANDIDATES CAMPAIGN AND HOLD DEBATES. ELECTIONS ARE HELD IN NOVEMBER, AND THE ELECTORAL COLLEGE CASTS VOTES IN DECEMBER.

THE HISTORY OF CAMPAIGNS

Presidential campaigns have existed since the first contested race in 1796, when John Adams and Thomas Jefferson both wanted to lead the country. (The nation's first president, George Washington, ran unopposed in 1789 and 1792.) The **rhetoric** was strong even when the country was

MAKING HISTORY

VICTORIA WOODHULL WAS THE FIRST WOMAN TO RUN FOR PRESIDENT OF THE UNITED STATES. SHE CAMPAIGNED UNDER THE EQUAL RIGHTS PARTY IN 1872. SHE ALSO WAS A STRONG SUPPORTER OF WOMEN'S RIGHTS, INCLUDING WOMEN'S RIGHT TO VOTE. IN 1904, GEORGE EDWIN TAYLOR BECAME THE FIRST AFRICAN AMERICAN TO RUN FOR PRESIDENT. HE WAS A JOURNALIST AND THE SON OF A SLAVE. HE RAN UNDER THE NATIONAL NEGRO LIBERTY PARTY.

GEORGE EDWIN TAYLOR

In 1872, Victoria Woodhull was the first woman to run for president of the United States.

young. The two sides in 1796 were the Republicans and the Federalists. The Republicans called for more democratic practices and accused the Federalists of **monarchism**. The Federalists accused the Republicans of supporting a radical, or extreme, group in the French Revolution.

There was one major difference between campaigns back then and current campaigns. In 1796, electors cast two votes for president, and the candidate who won the second most votes became vice president. Today, candidates for vice president campaign with presidential candidates.

While there were two sides in the first **contested** election, formal parties did not exist until 1828, when Andrew Jackson ran against John Quincy Adams. The Democratic-Republicans, or Democrats, developed the first **sophisticated** national network of party organization. This party held parades, barbecues, and other local events to promote its candidates. The challengers, the National Republicans, did not do this, but the party had a stronger platform.

The first woman to be nominated by a major party in a presidential election was Hillary Rodham Clinton. She accomplished this in 2016—around 227 years after the first president, George Washington, was elected.

POLITICAL PARTIES

BESIDES THE DEMOCRATS AND THE
REPUBLICANS, THERE ARE SEVERAL
OTHER PARTIES. SOME INCLUDE THE
CONSTITUTION PARTY, DEMOCRATIC
SOCIALISTS OF AMERICA, THE
GREEN PARTY, THE INDEPENDENT
PARTY, THE LIBERTARIAN PARTY,
AND THE REFORM PARTY.

Today, the main political parties are the Democrats and Republicans. Most presidential candidates have been white men. It wasn't until 2008 that a black man, Barack Obama, was elected president. And in 2016, Hillary Rodham Clinton, became the first woman nominated by a major party in a presidential election.

USE OF TECHNOLOGY

When we hear the word "technology," we often think of computers and social media. Barack Obama was the first candidate to use social media to spread his campaign message. Also, Donald Trump's use of Twitter, Instagram, and Facebook helped him to reach millions of people at one time during his campaign.

How did candidates campaign before social media? In 1836, William Harrison was the first presidential candidate to use passenger trains to travel around the country to deliver his campaign message. Also, in 1896, William McKinley was the first presidential candidate to use motion pictures for campaign purposes. And while you may be used to television now, in 1960, John F. Kennedy and Richard Nixon agreed to appear in the first televised presidential debate.

As technology has changed throughout history, presidential campaigns adapted. This was necessary to reach larger audiences. Few believed Barack Obama had a chance of becoming president. He was able to win, in part, because he mastered the use of social media to directly interact with voters.

WHAT CAN GO WRONG?

Sometimes presidential campaigns do not go as planned. In 1960, Richard Nixon was leading his race when he agreed to debate John F. Kennedy in the first live television debate. After the debate, voters thought Nixon looked uncomfortable and sickly. Voters also thought Kennedy looked young and passionate. Television led voters to consider how a candidate looked in addition to what a candidate thought. Kennedy became president. Nixon later became president in 1968 and again in 1972. A scandal during his 1972 campaign forced him to resign his presidency in 1974. The scandal involved members of Nixon's reelection campaign breaking into the offices of the Democratic National Committee in the Watergate complex in Washington, D.C. Nixon helped to cover up the crime.

PATH TO THE PRESIDENCY

FOUR U.S. PRESIDENTS WERE ASSASSINATED, OR KILLED, WHILE THEY WERE IN OFFICE. THEY WERE ABRAHAM LINCOLN (1865), JAMES GARFIELD (1881), WILLIAM MCKINLEY (1901), AND JOHN F. KENNEDY (1963).

In 1960, John F. Kennedy took the lead over Richard Nixon after the two agreed to participate in the first televised presidential candidate debate. Voters thought that Nixon appeared uncomfortable on TV, which hurt his campaign. This debate increased focus on the physical appearance of candidates.

CIVIC RESPONSIBILITIES

Presidential campaigns are only successful if everyone participates in the process. Candidates run for the chance to lead the country and influence the creation of new laws. Also, citizens have civic duties, or obligations, that they must perform. Some of these duties include obeying the law, paying taxes to fund the government, serving on a jury, staying informed, and voting. In a democracy, voting is very

Voting is every citizen's civic duty. You must be 18 years old or older to vote, but some states allow voters to register when they are 17. Rules are different in each state.

important. Voting ensures that democracy is maintained. Many people run for president every election cycle. For the 2016 campaign, there were more than 20 candidates! For the same election, only 61.4 percent of registered voters cast a vote. Without presidential candidates running for office, and without the people's ability and willingness to vote, we would not have a democracy.

WHAT WE HAVE LEARNED

Presidential campaigns are necessary in order for candidates to tell Americans why they should lead our country. Campaigns help candidates to raise and spend money so they can advertise their messages and travel around the nation to talk to voters. Candidates spend millions of dollars on campaigns. They also spend a lot of time on campaigns. The campaign season begins more than a year before the election. The candidate who eventually becomes president must win a primary election as well as the general election.

Campaigning has changed throughout history. The invention of television and the Internet allowed candidates to share their platforms with larger audiences. Without campaigns, voters would not know who the presidential candidates are. This is why presidential campaigns are important.

GLOSSARY

accountable: Responsible for your own actions.

advocate: Someone who supports a cause or idea.

contested: Disputed or made the object of competition.

crusade: A series of actions to advancing an idea or tending toward a certain end.

democracy: A form of government in which power is given to and exercised by the people or their elected leaders.

governance: The way a city or country is controlled by the leaders who run it.

immigration: The act of immigrating, or going to a country where one was not born.

inaugurated: Commenced officially; sworn in or administered an oath to.

monarchism: A belief in a monarchy, or a ruler who inherits authority, as a political system.

platform: A public statement of the principles, objectives, and policies of a political party.

preliminary: Something that comes before something else.

rhetoric: Loud, confused, and empty talk.

sophisticated: Complex or complicated.

WEBSITES

Due to the changing nature of Internet links, PowerKids Press has developed an online list of websites related to the subject of this book. This site is updated regularly. Please use this link to access the list: www.powerkidslinks.com/uspe/campaigns